Long Ago

S0-ANR-410

Written by Margie Burton, Cathy French, and Tammy Jones

Here is a house
from long ago.

Here is a house today.

Here is the inside of
a house from long ago.

Here is the inside of
a house today.

Here is a school from long ago.

Here is a school today.

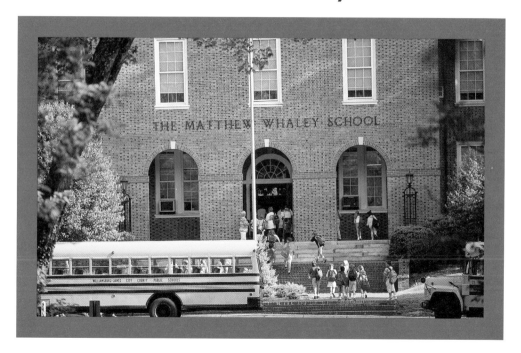

Here is the inside of
a school from long ago.

Here is the inside of
a school today.

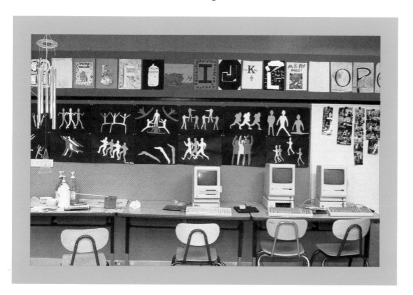

Here is a family from long ago.

Here is a family today.

Here are children from long ago.
They are playing.

Here are children today.
They are playing.

Long ago people had wagons.

Today people have cars.

Is this from long ago or today?